Making Money – Guid Can Be a BadAss Intelligent Investment Manager

Unshakeable Life Changing Financial Strategies for the Wealthy Intelligent Investor

Written by a Former Wall Street Firm Investment Banker and Chartered Wealth Manager ®

By: George Mentz, JD, MBA, CWM®

Table of Contents

Chapter 1 – Wealth Management 2.0 – The Fundamentals

When thinking about their financial future, today's families have much more to worry about than previous generations did. Modern families must carefully examine where they are in life and decide what types of investment tools and financial planning strategies they should use, including risk management and insurance options.

I remember a young man that I knew with two small children who was fatally electrocuted while doing some landscape work about two years ago. Sadly, and for reasons unknown, he had done little financial planning, and his family was left financially unprepared for his death. They needed a place to live, they needed a good education, and they needed to be able to meet all of their long-term financial goals, including healthcare and education for the children. We all know that 25-year-olds in good health are to approach because mortality is not on their minds, even with a spouse and two small children. While they may be on a tight budget, they may only need to set aside a few hundred dollars per year for a great insurance policy. If you can get them on board with you for risk management, and they continue to grow their businesses and families, you can develop good clients for life.

If something happened to that client, his family would be eternally grateful to you for the service that you provided. If his spouse received a tax-free million-dollar death benefit on a term-life policy—not even a whole-life policy, just a term policy—she could pay herself $50,000 per year for the next 20 years, or she could stretch the benefits to $25,000 per year for the next 40 years—even assuming no growth in principal. Insurance—and the lack of insurance in the face of an unexpected loss—can change the lives of your clients and their families.

Having been involved in wealth management for many years at a Wall Street firm, I have helped some of our most successful clients use insurance products to develop strategies that will protect their businesses and personal assets. Every family, regardless of wealth, needs some type of insurance to manage their risk. They may need health insurance, life insurance, homeowners insurance, and disability insurance. Wealthy clients may have other needs, such as special disability policies or succession planning policies for their businesses.

The use of insurance products for risk management is an integral part of wealth management that touches on all components of financial planning, including strategies for saving, investing, tax avoidance, retirement, and estate planning. Every major part of financial planning and wealth management contains risk-management needs that cannot be overlooked.

What I'm trying to explain in this book is that all of your clients can benefit from what you have to offer. People are busy today, and time is of the essence. If you can help your clients from beginning to end by putting together the paperwork, completing the forms and getting the testing done with added value and genuine concern for their lives, you will develop clients for life who will send you great referrals for the rest of your career.

Chapter 2: Guide to Wealth Preservation and Risk

As mentioned in the previous chapter, insurance and risk management is a subset of almost everything that we do in our financial lives. Insurance defends your clients and their families from catastrophic loss, and ensures that they have the resources to meet their needs for proper education, healthcare, and living expenses.

I grew up in the sixties and seventies, and I distinctly remember one family who lost their father in an accident. Fortunately they had a double indemnity clause that applied to the accident that took their father. In 1970, $1 million was a small fortune, particularly in a small town, and it could be used in creative ways to take care of the surviving family members. If the money was properly invested and protected in a prudent way, it would continue to grow and provide for his family forever.

Insurance can be used in all of the components of a financial plan. Let's start with investments. Both variable annuities and whole-life permanent insurance policies have an investment component. Variable annuities are non-taxable entities that continue to grow while they are in force, and your clients do not have to include that growth as income when they file taxes because it is growing tax-deferred. That growth can be an investment component in your client's financial plan. With permanent insurance such as whole-life, the cash value should grow over time and can also help to pay the premiums. When the insured dies the remaining value of the policies can pass to the beneficiaries, and may have tax implications.

The next component is retirement. Annuities, as well as other types of insurance, can be used as a retirement tool, too. For instance, if something happens to you, disability insurance could protect you throughout your working career until a designated age. When you retire, you may still receive money depending on what the terms of the policy.

Every Financial plan should consider estate planning. As a financial planner for the last two decades, I have typically seen insurance used to protect the companies and assets of the client's estate after death. The laws on estate taxes have changed dramatically in the last few years, and for sales purposes, you should consider the total net worth of an individual. Each individual in the United States has $5 million that they can leave in their estate before federal estate taxes start to kick in (an allowance that applies to each spouse). While a couple with a net worth of $10 million, may not have the same problems that they would have faced several years ago, you can think of every client, every person you approach, no matter how rich or how poor, as an estate planning client. Why? Two recent well-publicized examples can help us understand how these issues can affect our clients.

Sadly, Paul Walker, a handsome movie star, recently died with an estimated $20+ million net worth that he left entirely to his daughter. This generosity is noble and good, but without a proper risk mitigation plan and estate planning strategies, it may benefit government more than his daughter. $20 million, with a $5 million exclusion, leaves $15 million taxed at the highest rates. One can only assume that the federal and state governments would receive over $7.5 million of the Mr. Walker's estate. Similarly, Philip Seymour Hoffman's estate may owe more than $15 million in taxes that his three children will never see. Apparently, Hoffman's will was written before he had his last 2 children and since he was not married, the estate is taxed immediately rather than after the spouse passes away.

The next component of financial planning that relates to insurance is tax and taxation. If someone buys term life insurance or if someone buys whole-life insurance, a death benefit is paid to the designated beneficiaries when the insured dies. Every insurance policy specifies at least one beneficiary, and may also specify secondary beneficiaries and contingent beneficiaries. The benefits are passed directly to the beneficiary outside of probate, and can be taxable, but are often non-taxable. With each individual being able to leave $5 million tax-free, typically what you leave in insurance death benefits is going to be tax-free, even if it's to a child or a grandchild. Under the marital deduction rules, surviving spouses receive everything without any taxation. So, if a $10 million insurance policy goes to your spouse, it will not be taxed under the marital rules.

Finally there's the risk management part of financial planning that we've been talking about from the very beginning. Clients and their families all have different dynamics. The important thing is finding the decision maker who will be buying the insurance for the family. Sometimes it might be two decision makers. Do the analysis to find out how much coverage they need so that they can sleep well at night, knowing that they can protect their loved ones from some type of catastrophic event or health problem that might lead to death or permanent disability.

Whether you're selling term insurance or a combination of term and whole life to your clients, you're helping them protect themselves and their family. Every professional is going to need various types of insurance such as homeowner's insurance, an umbrella policy, policies for their automobiles and other vehicles, and disability protection. All of that requires tender loving care and value-added assistance from a professional to walk each client through the process, fill out the paperwork, get all of the required information, do the coverage analysis and then process the right policy for that particular client.

Chapter 3: PR, Credentials and The Business of Advising

Where are you in your life on an educational level? Are you up to speed with your knowledge on finance, investments, retirement tax and estate planning? The question of the day really is just like Dr. Steven Covey used to say in his famous book, *The Seven Habits of Highly Effective People*: "Are you sharpening your saw?" In other words, are you staying sharp? Before entering the investment world, a lot of people may already have a degree in finance, an

MBA, or some other well-recognized credential. The Chartered Financial Consultant is a great designation that was started by the American College many years ago. If you haven't taken the courses to obtain one of these designations, it's probably a good idea that you do so. Even if you've taken the basic insurance exam or the basic stockbroker's exam, they really don't prepare you for the dynamic of a high net-worth individual or an aggressive business professional.

A typical business person who's been in business for ten, fifteen, or twenty years and built a multi-million dollar company knows a lot about estate planning, taxes, financial planning, insurance and investments because they've put them together for their own business. These are smart people, and these are the people that you want to do business with. You need to be prepared to have a discussion on an equal footing with this type of top client.

The Pareto Principle states that 80 percent of your business comes from 20 percent of your clients. You are looking for are real, bona fide clients that can be partners with you in success. These are people that need your help, and can also grow your business. You are looking for young families who are just starting out and need to insure their lives, homes, or automobiles, or clients with growing businesses that need business insurance, or even families that are already wealthy, and have future generations of children and grandchildren to consider. Putting together a portfolio of these types of clients will help you grow your business.

When it comes to time management and prospecting, it's just as challenging to sell a $100,000 life insurance policy as it is to sell a $2 million life insurance policy, so it's all about client management. What type of clients do you want to work with, who do you want to do business with? You need to keep asking yourself that question. Who do you *really* want to do business with? Who is your ideal client?

So let's roll up credentials with time management and the type of people you want to work with. How do you want to present yourself? Who do you want to be? You have to start thinking about who you want to be. Do you want to be known as the top financial planner for small businesses? Do you want to be known as the guy who can put together the insurance trusts for wealthy clients? Do you want to be known as someone who can package it all together and make sure your services can protect a niche group of wealthy professionals, like lawyers and doctors? Do you want to help your clients with problems like estate planning and protecting their surviving spouses in case of death or disability?

For example, I know a doctor who had a great disability policy and couldn't practice medicine after being hurt in an accident, so he went into insurance sales. He became one of the biggest producers in the United States year after year because he was able to target doctors and other professionals with his story. His success was convincing because it was so personal. He could show people the scar on his neck and explain how his disability policy protected his family from bankruptcy and protected his children's future. He had a passion and desire to help other people and this doctor wanted to stay productive in life. Through his success he was able to help hundreds, if not thousands of people, and when some of his clients became injured or disabled they were able to have that same protection.

We need to keep our saws sharpened and stay current on changes that affect our clients and the products we recommend. Federal and state laws regarding taxes and insurance are always changing and we need to have access to the right education, the right books, and the right continuing education to be prepared for those changes.

National Underwriter and Summit Professional Networks have great books on insurance planning, tax issues related to insurance, sales books and time management books that licensed professionals need to grow and build their practices On top of all of that, many companies offer textbooks and courses that lead to a financial planning credential. For example, I teach at the Thomas Jefferson School of Law, which offers a non-degree seeking program that accepts non-lawyers. Students can take courses in wealth management, portfolio management, asset management, tax planning, and other courses that can help you relate to and counsel high net-worth clients. Students who complete these courses can obtain a certificate from the law school and a wealth management designation from the Academy of Finance and Management.

Maintaining your education, leadership skills and sales skills are all important. Buy tapes, CDs, DVDs—whatever you can get your hands on. Zig Ziglar, the famous sales professional, used to say you need to prime the pump and you need to get it moving. You need to do what you have to do to make the best of yourself so you can start producing and help as many people as possible. If you can do that, they will help you in return.

Chapter 4 – Prospecting, Belief and Building and Empire.

Last year I authored an article that was published on the NASDAQ website (available at http://news.efinancialcareers.com/us-en/11136/protecting-your-web-cred-from-hackers-whackers-and-reputation-hijackers/) about your credentials and your credibility on the internet, and how to maintain your image and reputation online. Twenty years ago all you needed to do was find a broker-dealer or an insurance company to sponsor you, work with them for a while to prove that you were a good salesperson, get your license, and go out there and start drumming up business. Nowadays it's a whole different world. First of all, the number of people selling financial products is a lot more than it used to be. Just think back in the mid-90s when Schwab started selling financial products and allowing trading online, and then all the other big players got into this business of offering financial advice and products at branches or directly online.

Today you have to build your credentials and your reputation in several key areas: in your community, online, within your profession, and with related professionals such as lawyers or CPAs. I wrote an article about using social media and internet search engine optimization to make sure your websites and social media activity pop up when people search for you. It's important to know that when people search for you and your credentials, they find out about you and the good things you have done, and not somebody else who they think might think is you. The key is to manage your image, manage your credibility, and manage your credentials. Make sure people know about you, your assets and your integrity. Our professional credentials are extremely important. You may have half a dozen letters behind your name, or maybe you haven't even finished college, but you have an insurance license and you are building a great practice. Regardless of who you are, most customers want someone who is knowledgeable about the products and services from beginning to end, and can explain the products and services that they offer to their clients.

I use the word "suitable" because that is the word that is used by the financial industry regulatory authority. What kind of credentials will help you be a better person? Financial planning courses from your local college or university, a law degree, an MBA, or a master's in financial planning are all great credentials to have. I personally have a law degree in international law, an MBA in financial planning, and additional coursework in tax and estate planning. I have passed the Series 7, and 63 exams as well as the Series 65 Investment Advisor Law exam. These credentials have given me a deep understanding of investments and insurance that I can demonstrate to my clients.

When I worked for a Wall Street firm I advised wealthy clients about their financial options. I would sit down with them and gather information piece by piece, just like a doctor, about their investments, retirement plans, insurance policies, brokerage statements, banking statements, wills, trusts and legal documents to find out what is going on with their financial lives. Then we would talk about their goals and time horizons and their retirement needs put together a suitable risk management package and financial plan. Ideally this plan will make these clients good customers in several different areas within your firm. The more ways that you can engage a client the more likely it is that they will stay with you. If you put together a good plan for someone and honestly show them how they can protect themselves and grow and preserve their wealth, then you will earn their respect and gratitude. The better you know your company's products, the more you can believe in them. If you believe in your products and services, you can sell confidently and seamlessly.

Chapter 4 - 40 Business Building Tips for Professionals

1. **Define your purpose.** Set one-year, three-year, and five-year goals. Create your public biography, and define the top 3 products and services you want to sell. Learn the details of each product and service inside and out. Learn the benefits and solutions that these products provide to your clients.

2. **Learn about social media.** Work with your compliance office to maximize your exposure on social networks. Learn to promote yourself aggressively in a way that is legal, fair and ethical. For a more detailed exploration of how you can enhance your online presence, see my article on "Protecting Your Web Cred from Hackers, Whackers and Reputation Hijackers" (available at http://news.efinancialcareers.com/us-en/11136/protecting-your-web-cred-from-hackers-whackers-and-reputation-hijackers/).

3. **Maximize your profile.** Illuminate your credentials, benefits and solutions to your customers in both print and online, as described in "Financial Careers and Strategy – The Art of Self Promotion" (available at http://www.advisorfyi.com/2012/04/financial-careers-and-strategy-the-art-of-self-promotion/).

4. **Remember friends and family.** If you have a friendly client, family member, or anyone to whom you have provided excellent service, always ask for referrals. Ask for 5 names of people who you can help. Remember the Rule of 250 – Zig Ziglar once said that everybody knows 200-250 people. It is said that at every funeral, the average person has about 250 friends, family, and colleagues show up.

5. **Think about who do you do business with.** For example: car dealers, banks, salons, local stores, and friends in your network can all be potential referral sources.

6. **Who do you want as your clients?** If you feel that your best way to do business would be to provide services to doctors only, then that may be your niche. As was discussed in Chapter Three, one of the top producers of disability insurance was a doctor who was disabled.

7. **Use Secretaries of State.** Each state has a website for its Secretary of State where you can find out who has registered a new business or trademark. Sometimes, these are people who need help with financial products and risk management.

8. **Think about your internal contacts.** If you are with a financial organization, find out if other departments that do not sell your products and services can refer clients to you.

9. **Use other types of professionals.** If you recommend lawyers, CPAs, or other professionals to your clients, be sure to ask those professionals for referrals.

10. **Use group presentations.** Ask if your local church or retirement home would like to have a free seminar on your products and services.

11. **Use electronic and print media.** Do a radio or TV show, or contribute to a local magazine or newspaper.

12. **Distribute newsletters.** See if you can build an email list or social media account to publish newsletters. Compliance content may even be available from your head office, so be sure and check with them first.

13. **Remember search engine targeting.** A website is good, but having your business presented in your community or zip code is important. Yahoo, Bing, Google and the rest allow for niche marketing using your preferred keywords and phrases which will attract the customers that you want.

14. **Get your brand name out.** Listing your business and name brand on the local sites is important. Submit your site, address, and phone to Google Local Results.

15. **Use Google.** Integrate your Google+ and Google Author Mode accounts with your website.

16. **Let your clients speak for you.** If you already have satisfied clients, ask them to recommend you on Angie's List, or other related consumer websites.

17. **Learn to use Pay Per Click (PPC) Advertising.** Microsoft, Google and Yahoo earn billions per year on internet ads. If these ads were not effective, people would not pay for them.

18. **Use separate lines of communication.** Use incoming phone lines and email accounts to track the success of your advertisements. These incoming numbers generally have no cost unless somebody calls you. Also, it is important to use dedicated email addresses for various types of ads.

19. **Join social network groups that are niche to your target market.** Facebook, Linkedin, and Yahoo have groups which you can join

that may contain people to whom you can provide solutions, services, and products.

20.   **Create a vignette video.** Short videos are awesome for sales people and professionals. The video can explain the benefits, procedures, and VIP treatment related to your products and services.

21.   **Create a booklet on "Questions to Ask Before you Hire an Estate Planner."** Give it away for free to those who provide an email address or phone number.

22.   **Benchmark your progress.** Make a list of the top five producers in your region. Search for them online and find out what they are doing to be successful.

23.   **Learn about PR services.** Online services can syndicate a press release for you for about 300 dollars. This can put your news and information in Yahoo News and many other websites. Be sure to promote your website, your email address and phone number in the press release.

24.   **Target an age group.** Some insurance professionals go to local graduate schools or medical schools and offer special informational seminars and one-on-ones to the graduates that discuss life insurance, disability and even malpractice insurance.

25.   **Target the less obvious.** Many times, you can gain the trust of executives and professionals by offering an analysis or checklist of their wealth management situation. There are many executives out there without things like an umbrella policy. This policy is cheap, and if your prospect does not have it, he or she may not think that their coverage is adequate.

26.   **Remember to cross-sell.** On most occasions, you can sell other products with your product. If somebody buys a suit, they would need a belt, tie, shirt and other accessories. The same idea is true for financial services. When "closing" your customer, don't forget to offer related products, services and benefits.

27.   **Offer beneficiary analysis to your clients.** One of the best practices is to sit down with a customer and find out how many policies and beneficiary related assets that they own and make sure they have

optimized their beneficiaries, contingent beneficiaries and secondary beneficiaries. Check their other accounts such as 401K, IRA, and other non-probate assets.

28. **Be a contributor.** The internet is a great way to hone your writing skills. You can always sign up on great websites to contribute your knowledge on risk, taxes, retirement, and customer satisfaction. It is also a great way to refer your clients to your authored articles. For example, www.ProducersWeb.com is a good place to write and publish content that your clients can see.

29. **Maximize your expertise.** Be a leader in your field and by maintaining updated books that can keep you fresh and on the cutting edge of relevant laws. This can impress your clients and you can teach them how to best use the law. Consider investing in *Tax Facts*, the *Field Guide to Estate Planning, Business Planning & Employee Benefits*, or the *Tools & Techniques of Financial Planning* from Summit Professional Networks.

30. **Offer planning services.** Offer your clients and your leads a detailed analysis of their retirement, tax, investments, insurance, budget planning, estate and college planning needs.

31. **Offer testing.** Offer your potential clients a physical so that they can get insured. If you want to sell big policies to prosperous clients, you need to make sure your blood and physical testing service is reliable, neutral and customer friendly.

32. **Review complaints.** Search online for complaints about other professionals in your field. Make sure you don't make the same mistakes that they did and take measures to avoid common problems.

33. **Ensure performance of your products.** Make sure you offer products and services with a good track record and performance. This enables you to respond to various questions by clients with positive feedback for long term success.

34. **Offer to do it for them.** Many top clients and prospects are really busy. Offer to gather all of the paperwork for them, fill out their details and get it ready. Provide VIP service and you can earn VIP compensation. Treat people and families like you would want your family to be treated.

35.   **Analyze the products that your clients already have.** Offer to review your clients' old policies. Sometimes the cash value of a policy has enough money to fund an entirely new policy with better protection for their families.

36.   **Look at using retirement dollars to fund insurance trusts.** Sometimes clients have an annuity or 401(k) that they can use to pull cash out to fund a new policy. Even if the client is under the age of 60, they may still be able to draw funds without penalty under section 72(t) of the IRS Code.

37.   **Review ownership issues.** Offer to analyze the ownership of each of your client's insurance policies for possible estate tax implications of owning a policy at the time of death.

38.   **Help your clients achieve lifetime income.** Offer your clients a lifetime of income with various annuity strategies. Funding a fixed income product for a spouse, child or grandchild can create regular income for life.

39.   **Know about and offer insurance trusts.** You can partner up with a lawyer and CPA to become a local expert on insurance trusts. This will help you be recognized as someone who can offer "turn-key" services for setting up trusts that can protect children, spouses, and future generations.

40.   **Write a Book.** Make the book about the top 3 services or products that you can use to help people. Check with your company your company to see if they already have a compliance-approved booklet or brochure that you can use. If not, you may be able to create a book and give it away to those who provide you with their contact information. The key is to build your network.

Chapter 5 – Your Internet Presence

If you are in the business of financial planning and insurance sales, your internet reputation needs to be in good shape regardless of whether you are in insurance, banking, brokerage, or lending. Nobody is excluded any longer, and the web does not discriminate.

What is "SEO REP?" It stands for "Search Engine Optimized Reputation." This means that the first pages of the search results for your company name and your personal name should produce results that are factual and to your advantage. In 2003, I published the first peer reviewed journal articles on search engine recruiting for colleges and universities.[1] Those journal articles stressed the importance of owning web property that is critical to your brand and mission, and those principles still hold true today. The newest challenge is social networking for business and the ownership web property that can be used for or against your interests on sites like Facebook, Linkedin, Google+ and Twitter. The challenge of "web real estate" is much bigger than it was ten years ago, and most of us will eventually need to have a presence on all of the major social and business networks.

Often, a CEO will purchase the domain name that represents their personal name, including the -.com, -.org, and -.net variations of their name spelling to claim it and protect it for factual promotion, as well as save it from vandalism. People who desire to have excellent SEO REP will also create accounts on all of the major social networks. To brand your own professional biography and information, keep updated accounts with the major job search engines. This will keep key web property from being taken hostage. Here are some other web properties where professionals would want to consider establishing an account for personal, company, or brand names:

- viadeo.com
- about.me
- ziggs.com
- businesscard2.com
- Myspace.com
- multiply.com
- emurse.com
- bigsight.org
- visualcv.com
- visible.me
- Wordpress

[1] See: Whiteside, R. & Mentz, George (2003). Online college recruiting and marketing: Web promotion, strategy, and ethics. *College & University*, *78*(3), 31-36., Mentz, G., & Whiteside, R. (2003). Internet College Recruiting and Marketing. *Journal of College Admission*, *12*, 10-17., and [1] Whiteside, R., Mentz George (2003), Online Admissions and Internet Recruiting: An Anatomy of Search Engine Placement, EDUCAUSE QUARTELY, Nr. 4, 63-66.

- gather.com
- ryze.com
- posterous.com
- peoplepond.com
- ziki.com
- flavors.me
- professionalontheweb.com
- publr.com
- Twitter
- bigsight.org
- Tagged
- Qzone (Chinese)
- Orkut
- MyLife
- Last.fm
- Hi5
- Friendster
- Flickr
- classmates.com
- BlackPlanet
- Bebo (India)
- Badoo (Latin American)
- Douban (China)

The list is dynamic and will continue to change. Should you create an account with each one of these sites? You can, and you might want to. After all, what if somebody else does it? What if your competitor claims your name? What if somebody claims a product name? Legally, there are very few effective protections against "name squatting" unless it is done in bad faith or they are using your copyrights and trademarks. Even then, it can be a hassle to try and get a domain turned over to you for a legal violation or have fraudulent content removed from any search engine results. Generally, personal names are not protected from being owned by others, so anybody can buy a domain name related to a real name and put up misleading information. Much like domain squatting, "social network squatting" is also a growing problem.

What can you do? There are "web credibility" services available for a fee that can help establish web properties related to your name and syndicate the information that you provide. You can do it yourself, but keeping a good reputation online requires time and money, and you may need professional help to ensure that sites with factual information are ranking well in the big search engines.

Taking action to control your personal, company and brand names may be necessary in the world of anonymous postings by competitors, crazy customers, old relationships gone bad, former employees, and former coworkers. Both a healthy sense of paranoia and a positive marketing strategy may be a good idea. Companies such as Reputation.com can also be consulted to begin a strategy to establish a larger web presence for you and your brand. If you are concerned about keeping a good name or worried about your SEO REP, open an account with Google or Yahoo and create some search alerts. These alerts will email you whenever somebody posts something about you that includes the keywords that you have included. If you need help, talk to an expert SEO consultant who has been in the business for a few years and decide if you should begin an active strategy to protect your name and your career.

Chapter 6 - Estate Planning – The Summary Analysis?

You may think estate planning is just for the wealthy. If your assets are worth one million dollars or more, estate planning is still an important and complex issue at both the federal and state level. With most assets such as homes and stocks devalued at the moment, those prices and valuations may move up quickly in the coming months and years. You should also be familiar with your spouse's net worth and pending inheritances.

With the tax changes in recent years, you may not need to worry so much about estate taxation because of the five million dollar cap under which an individual can bequest assets to his heirs without estate taxes. While the spousal exemption is still in force, but it will keep changing and taxes will probably go back up soon. For 2014 the exclusion amount will be $5,340,000 (which is up from $5,250,000 in 2013). However, the future of this exemption is always uncertain. Adding up the value of your assets can be an eye-opening experience. By the time you account for your home, investments, company value, retirement savings and life insurance policies you own, you may find your estate will end up in the taxable category, and you need to review all of the beneficiaries of 401Ks, annuities, or insurance policies.

You should consider whether to use the large exemption now and make large gifts of your holdings to your loved ones in the short term by prefunding insurance for children and grandchildren, transferring assets such as stock to loved ones (though you should be mindful of gift tax restrictions), or moving large gifts of family stock to your children. If you help your clients get their affairs in order, they will respect you. Also, it is always a good time for you or your clients to review:

1. Durable Powers of Attorney
2. Wills
3. Medical Directives
4. Trusts (Some may want to be voided and replaced)
5. LLCs and Company Stock (operating agreements)
6. State Tax issues
7. Guardianship designations
8. Use of a professional trustee
9. Beneficiaries designated in all of your insurance, annuities, or other non-probated assets.
10.   Document preservation.

The last challenge is document preservation. Make sure your important documents and policies are with a reputable law firm, trust department, in a bank deposit box that somebody knows about, or preserved in another type of lock box service that will notify your loved ones about your intentions. To truly protect wealthy clients, businesses, people, and property need to be insured properly. By doing this, you can protect the legacy of a family far into the future.

Chapter 7 - The Basics of Personal Risk and Loved Ones

It doesn't matter how rich, smart, or good-looking you are. Every one of us has certain risks that we have to take seriously as we go through our lives. As we mature, we become older and have expanding needs to protect our legacy and family. As prudent investors, we begin to purchase contracts or risk management insurance policies that will guard our family and our loved ones.

Various types of insurance can protect against the financial risk of dying or being temporarily or permanently disabled. Insurance can also protect your home, your occupation, your business, and your health. All of us have to realistically evaluate our families' financial needs.

You should ask every client two questions: First, can you afford not to have insurance? Second, how much insurance can you afford? If I was sitting down with your right now, the first thing I would say is: Do you have disability insurance? Do you have health insurance? Do you have homeowners insurance, car insurance and life insurance? And if so, where are your policies and can I see them because I need to know what they are about.

Of course every insurance contract, every policy has different terms regarding conditions, exclusions and deductibles. Once you are married, have a family, a business, or a certain amount of income things change dramatically. What is your family's "burn rate" for spending, and how does that change your ongoing needs? Everyone's profession and income are unique and some businesses can't be replaced or replicated. If you are a CPA or a lawyer or a doctor, your surviving spouse without those same credentials cannot take over that business and continue to run it if you are no longer able to.

How do we use insurance to protect ourselves and our families? The first thing you should ask a client is how is the surviving members of his family will replace his lost income to pay for their day-to-day needs. How are all those things going to be paid for? What about health care and educational expenses? Recently, I was talking to one professional, an insurance executive, and he said the expenses of sending his son to a good state college is costing him between $20,000 and $25,000 per year. Even in a bad economy, those costs are still rising with inflation. What about servicing debt, like a mortgage or credit cards? What type of taxes will be owed—local, state or federal—after you pass away? Then you need to think about who will take care of your children, if you aren't there anymore. Will your spouse continue to work, or do you want to buy enough insurance to guarantee that he or she will not have to work if something happens to you? Be sure to consider child care expenses, and upkeep for the home. Does your client have other responsibilities, such as caring for a spouse, child, or grandchild with special needs? Does your client have other complex situations involving a non-traditional family, such as divorce, two sets of children, or ongoing child support?

Moreover, there are various important business uses for life insurance, whether it's buy/sell agreements or business loans, executive benefits, or key person insurance. Imagine an insurance sales company with two partners in a small town. They're successful and have good revenue. One of them might want to buy insurance on the other person and vice versa. That way if one of them passes away, that way the surviving partner can buy out the surviving spouse if something happens to his business partner. It's just a typical buyout agreement that's funded with insurance. These policies are great. I've seen them work very, very well, particularly with the settlement of an estate because the cash is there.

Another issue to consider is ensuring that the surviving spouse and family has enough liquid assets on hand. I knew a family that owned a large company with a lot of stock, but when the patriarch of the family died, there wasn't enough cash available for his widow to settle the estates, provide a proper funeral, and pay all the bills. She had immediate needs, but not enough assets immediately available to protect herself from a difficult situation. It's always good for this cash to be available immediately, as is the case with a death benefit from an insurance policy.

The next issue to think about is children. Whether your client has two or ten children, insurance is probably one of the best ways to equalize benefits for kids and grandkids. Let's say you have five children of varying ages. You want to make sure the younger children have enough money to go to college while the older children have already graduated from college. You can control an insurance policy and make the primary beneficiaries of the death benefits to be the younger children where their amounts are a little bit larger than the other children. For example, the younger children might receive fifty percent of the insurance benefits or more and the older children might only get ten percent and the surviving spouse might get thirty or forty percent. You can also name grandchildren as contingent or secondary beneficiaries in case things change. You can use lots of strategies to distribute wealth to children and grandchildren with both term insurance and permanent insurance.

For developing new customers, another important issue is defining your target market or your "niche." Maybe you want to do business with millionaires. Maybe you want to do business with up and coming entrepreneurs. But consider that sometimes you're better off going after the younger executive who's still very healthy and you can talk to him about the benefits. If your customer is healthy now, you could issue some cost effective, quality insurance policies. You could provide a large insurance policy to a healthy thirty- or forty-year-old client than you can an older client. You could sell a combination of term and a combination of permanent insurance. Whether you're selling whole life or universal life, term or universal insurance, sitting across the table from a healthy client it makes the process a lot easier. You prepare them and get them in front of the right people to get the medical testing done, get the policy approved, and move forward to complete paperwork and get our customers under contract. Then they are committed to saving a certain amount of money to invest in themselves and improve their overall risk management program.

The beauty of having healthy clients or clients that have been screened and approved ahead of time is that you can offer several types of insurance. Once healthy clients are screened, you have a ready-made sales strategy. You can tell them that now is the time is now to get permanent, term, or disability insurance, all from the same great place. Now that you have the green light, you're able to get all of these policies under contract. What if something happens to them in a few months? If they are diagnosed with a serious long-term illness a year from now, the door of cost-effective insurance may be closed. That prospect may have friends or family who have been affected by medical conditions in their lives. They'll certainly understand your position regarding health and that time is of the essence.

The typical medium to high net-worth family may be bringing in a good amount of money each year, but they're spending most of it. The key is to get that client to dedicate a certain reasonable percentage of their income towards a risk management strategy that protects their surviving loved ones.

You may also focus on explaining to the prospect about how to protect himself against the risk of disability. And if he becomes disabled, the disability policies can pay for a certain standard of living and also pay other bills, including their other existing insurance policies. All of these things are possible, including tax-free disability payments from policies that are paid with after-tax dollars. Risk management and insurance is a vital part of every client's investment, retirement, and family wealth preservation strategies, and all of these areas need to be looked at very closely. And really, the highlight of insurance is that typically the death benefits that are paid to a spouse are tax free. Roughly the first $5 million of death benefits that are paid out of the estate are not taxed, and if you have an insurance trust set up for the benefit of your children, those benefits are completely outside of the estate after a few years. All of these things are vital ways to preserve and manage wealth while mitigating tax consequences.

Chapter 8 – Disaster Planning: Lessons from Hurricanes Katrina and Sandy

Clients like great tips to protect themselves and their family. As someone who was personally affected by Hurricane Katrina, I learned are many of the same lessons learned that most people around the world discover during natural disasters. The first is that survival is a priority, and you must take care of yourself and family first. If you endure a natural disaster, you can always rise up again if you work hard. The second lesson is that if you play your cards right, you can be ahead of the game. There are many ways to help your clients plan including: insurance, risk mitigation, home preparedness, equipment, business strategy, and contingency plans. Here are some areas to think about:

Information Technology and the Internet
Your clients' computers should be backed up. There are various companies that do this, and some services allow for you to have backup servers at other locations. Companies who survived the 9-11 attacks and hurricane Katrina were ahead of the competition in this regard. Further, we must all be wary of cyber-attacks also and use appropriate information security techniques.

Risk Management and Insurance

Most companies carry business interruption insurance, but flood insurance is also a good idea because most insurance policies do not cover "rising water" from flooding. The government sells affordable flood insurance to many Americans, but you must buy a contract well before a storm occurs to have coverage in force. Many great insurance companies are involved in business, home and rental insurance.

Equipment and Power

In addition to backing up data, consider using external hard drives, auxiliary power generators, and water proof safes to protect against water damage

Communications, Phone and Email

Maintaining communications after a storm is key, both with your customers and your employees. Many firms have employees that can work from anywhere as long as they have access to the company's servers and technology. Keep in mind that those wireless providers whose cell towers are still up become the default provider after a disaster. Also, social networks are extremely useful for group communications, news distribution, and sharing data.

Disaster and Hurricane Planning

If you are making a contingency plan, an online search for "Disaster Recovery Plan" can yield useful suggestions. While many people do know about risk, risk management is not a typical part of our education in college or in the workplace. Each employee or department or family member should have a role to play in emergencies. If you need expert help, then talk to a good management consulting firm.

Take Common Sense Action

Put hard-to-replace items such as family photos, personal computers or other collectibles in a safe place or on the second floor of the home if possible. If a natural disaster is predicted for your area, gas up the cars, bring your medicine, secure your property, have credit cards with you, book hotels out of town early, and evacuate sooner rather than later.

Be Aware of News and Current Events
Be prepared and stay aware. Weather websites such as weather.com and www.weatherunderground.com provide invaluable information both before and after an event. Use them to remain knowledgeable about what to do and what to avoid in the event of a natural disaster.

Document Your Damages
While most insurance companies deal in good faith, companies are not eager to pay out claims unless well substantiated. If your property is damaged, document it. Make a film of the property before and after, take pictures, and hire a consultant after the event to formulate the claims if necessary.

Other Disaster Variables
While many people do not worry about catastrophic events, these problems pop up when you least expect it. Whether it's the earthquakes of the early 1990s in California, the recent fires in Colorado, record tornados in the southeast, the earthquake and nuclear meltdown in Japan, flooding, blizzards, droughts, or even terrorism, unexpected risks can still be managed with the right strategies.

With many major cities less than forty feet above sea level, all families and business people should think carefully when planning for risk management or catastrophic events. While the federal government has a role to play in these incidents, Hurricane Katrina was a lesson that you as a professional must have a plan for your clients to assist in help with this risk. When Katrina devastated New Orleans, those with a plan and good insurance suffered the least injury.

Chapter 9 - The Psychology of The Rich and Top Financial Professionals

Throughout life, there is always a celebrated group of people who succeed and many of us who fail. What separates the two groups? As an avid researcher of success literature, there are many psychological, human potential, and even metaphysical strategies to improve our performance or reinvigorate our potential. The irony to life is that we will all need to continually expand our character and capabilities in any career that we engage.

To begin this discussion, let us start with the premise that all great sales success begins with an idea or plan. Many sales professionals become successful by using great planning and time management techniques. Thoughts and planning can turn into real results. Your ideas, combined with the appropriate desire and plans, are the basis of most success. A strong desire can bring your idea into a reality. If you began your business idea with the strong desire to grow and never look back, you probably are successful today if you maintained the persistence for continued growth. Planning is crucial because most people do not commit to or define what they will do, and are too timid to write down exactly what they want to achieve and how they will realize the goal in any degree of specificity.

Having definite objectives and a specific plan along with a strong desire for success is required to accomplish great things. A burning desire is something that you really want to do. Purpose allows you to take action on your burning desire and develop a plan. You should have faith that you can make your plan happen.

If you are willing to sever the past and move forward with your objectives and desires, new opportunities can open up. If you are willing to focus your attention and positive emotions almost exclusively on this career performance, and never give up, your success is guaranteed. Having your stated objectives written out while keeping a good attitude, enthusiasm, and persistence that is built on honesty and integrity will propel your business growth.

This section includes short bullet points that describe an easy path to defining your plan. This involves putting pen on paper to write out clearly what you want to achieve.

Be Purposeful and Specific:
Create a personal agreement with yourself by firmly establishing what you want. Write your plan in specific terms by determining:

- What you desire to accomplish (the specific contribution and amount of success or dollars that you want to earn and create)
- What effort, time commitment, and value that you will give to earn and deserve that outcome
- How you will conduct and arrange your life and business to allow the receipt of prosperity and compensation
- When you will achieved your goal
- Sign and date the written plan or contract with yourself
- Read the plan daily at the beginning and end of your workday.
- Believe that you have already achieved success in heart and mind and harvest that emotion of attainment.
- Imagine how you will help people and the benefits that they will have.
- Imagine what you will do with your success.

Enthusiasm and faith can be induced through several practices or exercises: Enthusiasm and a proactive attitude, when coupled with your desire, can propel a plan to great heights. As for the philosophical aspects of success, many professionals use these techniques for a few minutes every day to reaffirm their purpose, their personal faith, and their success attitude so that they will indeed accomplish what they desire.

1. Find a quiet spot to relax.
2. Read statements of your action plan or desire for sales success (think about your personal objectives in you "mind's eye").
3. Practice forming mental images of your personal success in your spare time. For example, imagine your potential clients thanking you for the service and insurance after you have closed the deal.
4. Project the image of your success on the subconscious mind using a heartfelt emotion. See that you have success already in your mind:

imagine yourself with a salary five times what it is today and feel the emotions of achieving that goal at year-end. We stress that you do this daily and imagine how you will use the success for the benefit of your family or business.

5. Read aloud the professional and successful attributes that you desire such as: "I am a great professional and deserve to have great clients."
6. Use gratitude and thankfulness of heart. Complaining and being negative is a waste of your time and energy. Moreover, when being thankful for your job, career, clients, health and so forth, you will create the energy of success that will bring you more positive outcomes, happiness, and confidence. Further, new clients and your existing clients will be attracted to your positive world view. Believe me, clients can sense this. You should contemplate the good in your life focus on how you can be excellent to yourself and others.
7. Combine the above steps with Action, Action and More Action. See Below.

A Successful Action Plan:

- Your actions must be persistent. This means that we should be proactive in building new business as well as keeping satisfied customers.
- Avoid lack of decision and procrastination, and stick with your decision and plan. For example, don't be afraid to let go of a bad client if managing this relationship isn't worth your time and energy.
- Write down each day what you will do to move forward with your business or sales plans. Be efficient and effective.
- Do all you can do each day without haste. Do not worry about yesterday or tomorrow. Today, you should accomplish all you can. Over time, this focused task management adds up, and you will receive positive results in your business.
- Strong thoughts of gratitude and enthusiasm will bring about change for the better in you and your environment. Focus on what you desire, on being the best, and thinking about the best for you, your family, and your business.
- Organize your affairs so that you can receive the rewards of a better business. Allow for new and better clients. Believe that you deserve them, and do not be afraid to charge them value for value. This may mean acquiring greater business tools, administrative assistance,

infrastructure use, and ways to capture income. This may entail offering a broader line of products or services. Be prepared to provide solutions and do the homework.

- Surround yourself with encouraging professional mentors or advisors. Find out what producers are doing and how they are doing it. Model yourself after the best.
- Know in your heart that great results in line with your persistent desires will come to you at the right time.

Seek Professional Growth and Mentors

Develop a group of friends who can give you professional insight and feedback, and will support your goals by sharing their own experiences and tactics. Be willing to help all members in this group of professional friends with your knowledge, skill, and support. Meet often for planning and to obtain and give feedback to your group. You must always speak and act to maintain harmony with this group with positive and encouraging conversation. Do not belittle or contradict your group members. Offer solutions, not criticism.

Belief in Yourself, Your Purpose and Service

Believe that your products and services are as good as or better than any products out there. Know the details of your products and services. Be able to articulate the benefits of your service. Chances are what you sell is just as good as what the competition offers, and your products and services create opportunity for clients. Do not be afraid to sign up a new business client because someone else will do this if you don't. Moreover, remember that some small clients take just as much time to manage as very large clients. Therefore, time management is essential. Over time, it is better to have twenty great accounts than 150 non-productive customers.

Being Successful

In my career, I have helped many people. I feel great joy in contributing to anyone's financial freedom. Moreover, I realize that many of you are great successes already and commend all of you. With success, there is usually hard work and many people who depend on you. As a reminder, there will be times when you just need to rest, relax, or take a vacation. There will be seasons where you may need to rejuvenate your enthusiasm for your business or even take some new courses. With all of that being said, your physical and mental wellbeing is the most important thing to maintain so that you may continue all of your good works. Therefore, try to keep a balance with body, mind and soul through good exercise, diet, leisure, and.

Remember that you are chosen and naturally unique
Whatever your background, believe that it is good. Regardless of your challenges in the past, believe that you can be better as you garner more knowledge and understanding of the laws of life. Regardless of your appearance today, you can be or look better, improve yourself, be healthy, and enhance your image in your own exceptional way. It does not matter what has happened in the past, your knowledge and awareness can be cultivated to a new dimension where peace of mind is yours.

I believe that everyone, including you, has been chosen to do great things and live a significant life. You have special given talents. You must allow your assets and skills to be honed and sharpened. Do not die with your vision and talents unused. You can be great, and you can make outstanding contributions to your family and to humanity. There is nothing wrong with being confident in who you are. Only good can come from growth. Sometimes change is difficult, but rebirth or reinvention is available to all. If you are ready to be the best, begin today.

Chapter 10 – Timeless Principles of Success

The pursuit of success is as old as civilization, and many ancient thought leaders promulgated lessons that are still relevant today. Below are some ideas from three of my favorite thinkers: Marcus Aurelius, Ben Franklin, and Sun Tzu.

Marcus Aurelius (121-180 AD)

Emperor Cesar Marcus Aurelius wrote the 12 Books of the Meditations as a source for his own guidance and self-improvement, and they have some great tips for business, spiritual balance, politics, and relationships. Much like the principles of the Art of War by Sun Tzu or Ben Franklin's 13 Virtues of character development, these insights from the warrior-general are designed to help the reader reach his or her potential. Marcus Aurelius was emperor of Rome and was notable among Roman emperors as he was a devotee to the study and practice of philosophy of Socrates, Plato, Alexander the Great and more. Here are the some Timeless Principles of Success from: Emperor Marcus Aurelius (all references are from *The Meditations of Marcus Aurelius*, translated by George Long. Vol. II, Part 3 of the Harvard Classics, New York: P.F. Collier & Son, 1909–14):

1. Look for the best in life. (Book 10, §1)

2. Acting with confidence and poise. (Book 3, §5)

3. Be and live your purpose and focus upon engaging your vision and mission. (Book 9, §19 and Book 10, §16)

4. Stay in the now and act in the present. (Book 8, §44)

5. The present is a gift. (Book 8, §44)

6. We must express ourselves naturally. Use your own style to be excellent but also use the most practical techniques. (Book 11, §13)

7.   Our greatest power is our choice and ability to control our thought - Choose not to be harmed and operate beyond the basic senses. (Book 4, §7)

8.   Go within to develop inner peace. Renew yourself, rest, meditate, and recharge. (Book 4, §3)

9.   Do your job with diligence, energy, focus and patience. (Book 3, §12)

10.   Be aware of the power within you and nurture it. This can include exercise, diet, rest, empowerment, and learning. (Book 2, §13)

11.   Projects can be broken down to tasks and achieved one at a time finishing each part with excellence. (Book 6, §26)

12.   Our every task is to be done in an excellent way and shine like a jewel of great wealth. (Book 7, §15)

13.   Be contemplative in action and listen to others to learn the best ways to respond. (Book 8, §5)

14.   No need to complain aloud or to yourself in mind. (Book 8, §9)

15.   The word attribute can mean to make a tribute, complement others' good works, and find acceptance and thankfulness outwardly. (Book 8, §23)

16.   Joy and memories are created. (Book 8, §25)

17.   Striving for the right view while repressing animal instincts (Book 8, §29)

18.   See past mere appearances. Try and go beyond what is apparent and see truth. (Book 12, §18)

19.   Focus on your purpose toward highest performance results while avoiding blame. (Book 12)

20.   Use what is available, maximize your talents, and take advantage of the things that are provided. (Book 8, §32)

21.   The imagination can lean toward negativity, but a constructive imagination in the now is very powerful. (Book 8, §36)

22.   Your soul takes the color of your thoughts. (Book 5, §16)

23.   Look at what you have, the things you value most and think how much you would crave them if you did not have them anymore. (Book 7, §27)

24.   Live your life as though today's actions will be remembered and you have one day left as a gift. Act and live without haste or sloth. (Book 7, §56)

25.   Change and impermanence are features of existence. Particularly that change is inevitable and that it should be embraced. (Book 9, §32)

26.   Give yourself time to learn something new and good, and cease to be whirled around. (Book 2, § 7)

27.   The Emperor stresses the importance to flow with the Universe and use its energy in your favor. (Book 8, §23)

Benjamin Franklin (1706-1790)

Benjamin Franklin was one of the founding fathers of the United States and was a leading author, politician, inventor, and diplomat. He sought to cultivate success and character in himself and others by using a methodology of thirteen virtues, which he developed in 1726 and continued to practice for the rest of his life. Franklin was a wise master, mystic, and much-loved ambassador. Franklin would reflect daily over his actions and character before going to bed in order to improve himself. Here is a customized version of Franklin's virtues of success (from *The Autobiography of Benjamin Franklin*. Philadelphia: H. Altemus, 1895):

1. "TEMPERANCE. Manage your behavior in a professional way."
2. "SILENCE. Speak with both purpose and skill, and only when needed."
3. "RESOLUTION. Resolve to perform with integrity and resolve."
4. "FRUGALITY. Invest in yourself and do not waste time."
5. CLEANLINESS. Respect of body, clothes, or home."
6. "MODERATION. Avoid extremes."
7. "INDUSTRY. Be engaged in activities that are purposeful; minimize unnecessary actions."
8. "SINCERITY. Be a constructive person who praises others; and, if you speak, speak professionally."
9. "JUSTICE. Keep your personal and business relations win-win where both parties benefit. Treat yourself and others with high regard
10. TRANQUILLITY. Be not distracted by the whims of society and focus on building your family, business and your customers.
11. "CHASTITY. Use your charisma in the right areas of your life."
12. "HUMILITY. Remain teachable and right sized."
13. "ORDER. Keep healthy routines with body, mind and spirit. Use planning to focus on building your character and helping people in each key area of their lives."

Sun Tzu (544-496 BC)

Sun Tzu was a Chinese general who is credited with *The Art of War*, a military strategy guide. Its principles are written broadly enough that many of them still apply to non-military struggles today. Below are some of Sun Tzu's timelessly relevant maxims, modernized for today's strategic risk management battles (from Lionel Giles' edition of *The Art of War* by Sun Tzu, 1910, Public Domain):

a) Laying Plans/The Calculations

Use a SWOT analysis for any situation or client. Look at the strengths, weaknesses, opportunities and threats for any business challenge or client.

b) Waging War/The Challenge

Know what you are willing to invest in with each client and know when move on to the next customer.

c) Attack by Stratagem/Planning Offense

All relationships should have a vision and mission. You should know what you will say, how to say it, know the customer, and be prepared to answer tough questions in relation to the clients individual needs.

d) Tactical Dispositions/Positioning

Each of us should know the right products and strategies for each unique customer to provide skill and diligence with our business activities.

e) Energy/Directing

Use your personal energy and charisma to help a client but also allow your team to assist you in any way that will allow your company be a unified team to assist people with risk and opportunity.

f) Weak Points & Strong/Illusion and Reality

Each client's situation, business, and family dynamic changes with time. Be prepared to assist customers with each new season by maintaining knowledge about your key customers.

g) Maneuvering and Dealing with Confrontation

Be prepared for tough customers, tough family members, spouses, and other non-traditional relationships. Empower decision makers to work with you.

h) Variation in Tactics/The Nine Variations

Be prepared to respond to shifting circumstances successfully.

i) **The Army on the March/Adapting**

With new laws and new government rules, all of us must stay apprised of the best products and services to match up with the right clients.

j) **Terrain/Situational Positioning**

Know your customer. Communicate with them the information they need to make informed decisions or utilize the benefits that you offer.

k) **The Nine Situations/Nine Terrains**

Understand the terrains of Finance, Risk, Financial Planning, Investments, Tax, Insurance, Banking, Economics, Retirement, Estates and Trusts.

l) **The Attack by Fire/Fiery Attack**

Use strategic tactics: Marketing, Time Management, Planning, Wealth Management, and more.

m) **The Use of Intelligence**

Competitive intelligence and benchmarking allow you to know your competition, know your customer, and know your target market.

Chapter 11 – Wealth Risk Management Summary

To sum it up, here are some of the golden keys to success in the insurance business and the relationship building business. I think every insurance professional should determine anywhere from three to five urgent and important things to do per day that will expand their business. I would encourage each professional to reach out to at least three to five people per day to set up appointments with those who you want to do business with.

When seeking appointments, I advise people to bring value to the table. Bring customer-centered information that can help them, and say, "I am willing to sit down with you at your convenience at my office, or at your office, and go over your wealth preservation plan and your insurance policies, but also go over some tips and some strategies that we offer that may be able to protect you even further and save you money."

Every relationship with your financial clients or insurance customers involves a wealth planning method and traditional project management processes. You should interview each client to investigate his total financial situation and determine what's going on in his career and family at this particular juncture. Analyze that information to develop a plan to protect their assets. After you initiate that plan, continue to monitor the plan's performance while looking for opportunities for improvement.

Along the way don't forget about confidentiality issues, suitability requirements, and the "know-your-customer" rules. Understanding your clients' needs is job number one. After you find out what they already have and what they need, you might be able to fill in some gaps or be able to prepare them for the next cycle of their life and give them the proper protection from risk.

 "Suitability" is something that is important in the legal world and also in the financial regulatory world. It means that all the products and services that you are offering should be adequate or are suitable for the actual customers that you have. For an example, you don't want to take some 401(k) money from a retiring client who's in his late sixties and roll them over into a variable annuity and put them into all high-techs stock mutual funds or exchange traded funds because that would put their retirement savings at a risk because that is not prudent or reasonable.

You should also review all of the client's relevant documents to the extent possible. Review wills and the trusts accurately to make sure that you are providing an appropriate service or a product considering the details of that will or trust. For high net-worth deals, you may need to involve an attorney or a CPA to make sure that all of the i's have been dotted and the t's have been crossed.

There are behind-the-scenes issues such as getting the right products and the right rated companies for your customers so that you can offer them what they need within an acceptable price range. You want to be able to offer great products that help your clients, but compensate you and your company fairly, as well.

It is all about a win/win deal. If you're offering great advice, great services and great products then you deserve to be paid, particularly since you're acting as a high net-worth risk management professional. You're trying to get everybody to the table, and get the deal done. Make sure everyone involved gets the documentation that they need, including the client, attorney, CPA, and family members. Instruct your clients and their family members to keep their copies in a safe place.

Great sales executives and leaders will convey the impression of success to their customers, making them understand and that you're a person who can deliver excellent service and excellent products, which provide value to your clients. Your ability to explain your products and services clearly will bring extra professionalism to the table by saying "Here are the benefits of what I have to offer. Here's how it's going to help you. Can you afford not to have it? Here's the value that I'm bringing." To be of service, sit down with your clients, investigate what's going on, diagnose and put together a plan for them and their families, explain it, work with their other financial advisors, lawyers, or CPA's to initiate this plan, monitor it, and continuously improve on it.

Most financial advisors, stock brokers, portfolio managers, and hedge fund guys can't sell insurance. You're the licensed professional. You're the person who's going to be able to put the risk management products and services in front of these people, and if you're lucky you may be able to cross-sell them after you've booked them into some great products and services that protect them with great benefits. After that, you might be able to ask them for more business. Do they have old 401(k)'s that you want to rollover? Do they want to invest in tax-differed variable annuities where the money is going to grow tax-free? There are many other ways you can cross-sell and help your clients preserve their wealth to stay prosperous.

Study the small book well. Take the suggestions that you like and implement them into your life plan. Commit to your goals and desires. Become a leader of excellence and be the best provider of risk management services. Build and maintain your edge and you will be known in your community as the person who provides solutions and peace of mind.

"If one advances confidently in the direction of his dreams and endeavors to live the life which he has imagined, he will meet with a success unexpected in common hours."

- Henry David Thoreau

Appendix 1 – The Garden – A Story of Planting Seeds and Sales Growth

1. **G is for Good and God** – Know that if you enter the garden and begin your work, that the universe and life force will allow you to farm your good and reap what you sow.
2. **A is for Attention and Atonement** – If you are willing to clear away the debris in your garden, till it, weed it, and make it a place that is conducive to growth, then your mental garden will be ready for seeds.
3. **R is for Ready to Receive** – Clear the garden, and ready the mind to receive new and good seeds, plants and crops.
4. **D is for Decide** – You must select the seeds, the best for the climate and season. You must commit to planting and putting them into the right place to receive sunshine, light, nutrients, and rain.
5. **E is for Emotionalize and Efforts** – You must put your feelings behind your work and your seeds/ideas. These ideas have been planted, and now it is time to back the ideas up with action, boldness, joyful effort, and enthusiasm.
6. **N is for NOW** – You clear the weeds in the now, you plant the seeds in the now and you nourish the garden in the now, you protect the garden in the now, you let go of the process and allow the seeds to grow in the now, and we harvest in the now. We have a plan in the now, and we execute. We have the prospects willing to be satisfied and we deliver. The recipient happily rewards our joyful efforts.

Appendix 2- The 12 Characteristics of Proactive People

1. **A purpose driven personality** with a desire to express themselves in the most constructive ways.
2. **A worldview and consciousness of possibility,** prosperity and harmlessness
3. **People who are beyond competitive and very creative.** Visionaries who strive to see and feel the reality of their dreams.
4. **Gratitude minded** – people with a thankful heart and sincere belief in the goodness of the universe.
5. **Boldness, action oriented**, willing to take calculated risks, and Authentic.
6. **Self-regard** – people who believe that they are worthy of a rich and full life and are willing to work to receive it.
7. **At ease with a harmonious mind and thoughts**. People willing to cultivate peace of mind and balance in body, mind and spirit.
8. **Love of fellowship** – willing to help others with time and talent.
9. **Receptivity** - Global & Nonjudgmental openness to others' ideas and creativity. Open to inspiration.
10. **A Unique spirit** – Individualization of soul and spirit. Allowing yourself to become who you are meant to be.
11. **Desire to serve humanity** by being your best. A passion to contribute as an individual to the greater good.
12. **Consciously awake** - People who have become spiritually awake to a higher order of being and work to maintain such a level of thinking, acting and being.

Appendix III - The Master Key List – The Plan

Begin your new life today. Write out 5, 10 or even 50 things that you want to do to improve your life and circumstances. Don't be shy! Write the amazing and exciting things you will achieve about money, travel, relationships, health or whatever. Do it and do it today. As the great poet von Goethe once implied, Begin it TODAY and there is MAGIC and POWER in it.

Write out your Master Key List and put it in your pocket. Think about it for a day. Then pick the 3 most important things you can do to change your life for the better and begin immediately to commit to those 3 goals.

Every day, when you are in your Alpha Relaxed State, you can read the list to yourself. Read it at night and upon awakening. Think about the completed successes. Think about the ESSENCE of your purpose and how you can help yourself, your family and others by attaining your dreams.

As part of your continual growth, you can enhance, add, expand and remove things from your Master Key List.

Reasons for the List:

1. Codify in your sub-conscious the things that are important to you.
2. Allow for your mind to visualize and prepare for the objective
3. Begins the act of Boldness or Commitment to a goal
4. Forces you out of your comfort zone.
5. Gives you purpose and rationale to your ideas.

*Taken from to Book It Works If You Work It

It Works If You Work It - The Power of Success: The Greatest Success Secrets Ever Known by: George Mentz, JD, MBA

Cheat Sheet for Taxes 2015

For tax year 2015, there are annual inflation adjustments for more than 40 tax provisions, including the tax rate schedules, and other tax changes. The tax items for tax year 2015 of greatest interest to most taxpayers include the following dollar amounts. Keep in mind that the AFA Affordable Care Act will increase many taxes on capital gains, income, and other areas including reducing tax deductions for high income earners and families.

• **Income Tax Rates:** The tax rate of 39.6 percent affects singles whose income exceeds $413,200 ($464,850 for married taxpayers filing a joint return), up from $406,750 and $457,600, respectively. The other marginal rates – 10, 15, 25, 28, 33 and 35 percent – and the related income tax thresholds are described in the revenue procedure.

• **Standard Deductions:** The standard deduction rises to $6,300 for singles and married persons filing separate returns and $12,600 for married couples filing jointly, up from $6,200 and $12,400, respectively, for tax year 2014. The standard deduction for heads of household rises to $9,250, up from $9,100.

• **Personal Exemptions:** The personal exemption for tax year 2015 rises to $4,000, up from the 2014 exemption of $3,950. However, the exemption is subject to a phase-out that begins with adjusted gross incomes of $258,250 ($309,900 for married couples filing jointly). It phases out completely at $380,750 ($432,400 for married couples filing jointly.)

• **Retirement Accounts:** The elective deferral (contribution) limit for employees who participate in 401(k), 403(b), most 457 plans, and the federal government's Thrift Savings Plan is increased from $17,500 to $18,000 in 2015. See other rules on retirement accounts at the IRS. For 2014, workers age 50 and older can contribute an additional $5,500 to their 401(k) in 2014, or a total of $23,000. For 2015, it is $6000 catch up and 18,000 contribution for a total of 24,000 thousand dollars.

• **Estate Tax:** Estates of decedents who die during 2015 have a basic exclusion amount of $5,430,000, up from a total of $5,340,000 for estates of decedents who died in 2014. Please discuss with a lawyer regarding portability or state taxes.

• **Foreign Income:** For 2015, the foreign earned income exclusion breaks the six-figure mark, rising to $100,800, up from $99,200 for 2014.

• **Gifting:** The annual exclusion for gifts remains at $14,000 for 2015.

• **FSA:** The annual dollar limit on employee contributions to employer-sponsored healthcare flexible spending arrangements (FSA) rises to $2,550, up $50 dollars from the amount for 2014.

Under the small business health care tax credit, the maximum credit is phased out based on the employer's number of full-time equivalent employees in excess of 10 and the employer's average annual wages in excess of $25,800 for tax year 2015, up from $25,400 for 2014.

• **Added Capital Gains Taxes With ACA (AKA) Obamacare:** The Net Investment Income Tax is imposed by section 1411 of the Internal Revenue Code. The NIIT applies at a rate of 3.8%. Individuals will owe the tax if they have Net Investment Income and also have modified adjusted gross income over the following thresholds:

Filing Status	Threshold Amount
Married filing jointly	$250,000
Married filing separately	$125,000
Single	$200,000
Head of household (with qualifying person)	$200,000
Qualifying widow(er) with dependent child	$250,000

Taxpayers should be aware that these threshold amounts are not indexed for inflation. If you are an individual who is exempt from Medicare taxes, you still may be subject to the Net Investment Income Tax if you have Net Investment Income and also have modified adjusted gross income over the applicable thresholds

• **Capital Gains:** The tax rate on most net capital gain is no higher than 15% for most taxpayers. Some or all net capital gain may be taxed at 0% if you are in the 10% or 15% ordinary income tax brackets. However, a 20% rate on net capital gain applies in tax years 2013 and later to the extent that a taxpayer's taxable income exceeds the thresholds set for the new 39.6% ordinary tax rate ($406,750 for single; $457,600 for married filing jointly or qualifying widow(er); $432,200 for head of household, and $228,800 for married filing separately). See more on capital gains at the IRS.

• **Qualified Dividends:** Are the ordinary dividends subject to the same 0%, 15%, or 20% maximum tax rate that applies to net capital gain. They should be shown in box 1b of the Form 1099-DIV you receive. The maximum rate of tax on qualified dividends is:

-
  o 0% on any amount that otherwise would be taxed at a 10% or 15% rate.
  o 15% on any amount that otherwise would be taxed at rates greater than 15% but less than 39.6%.
  o 20% on any amount that otherwise would be taxed at a 39.6% rate. See more on qualified dividends at the IRS.

• **Deduction Limits:** The limitation for itemized deductions to be claimed on tax year 2015 returns of individuals begins with incomes of $258,250 or more ($309,900 for married couples filing jointly).

• **Health Care Tax Penalties:** The Affordable Care Act mandates that all Americans have health insurance, or pay a tax penalty as a result. In 2015, penalties ramp up to 2% of total household income, or $325 per person – whichever is greater.

• **AMT (Alternative Minimum Tax):** Exemption amount for tax year 2015 is $53,600 ($83,400, for married couples filing jointly). The 2014 exemption amount was $52,800 ($82,100 for married couples filing jointly).

• **EITC:** The 2015 maximum Earned Income Credit amount is $6,242 for taxpayers filing jointly who have 3 or more qualifying children, up from a total of $6,143 for tax year 2014. The revenue procedure has a table providing maximum credit amounts for other categories, income thresholds and phaseouts.

Quotes on Prosperity and Abundance

- "Wealth is not his that has it, but his who enjoys it." —Benjamin Franklin

- "Life is a field of unlimited possibilities." —Deepak Chopra

- "He who is plenteously provided for from within, needs but little from without." —Johann Wolfgang von Goethe

- "Take full account of the excellencies which you possess, and in gratitude remember how you would hanker after them, if you had them not." —Marcus Aurelius

- "Whenever anything negative happens to you, there is a deep lesson concealed within it, although you may not see it at the time." —Eckhart Tolle

- "If you want to change who you are, begin by changing the size of your dream. Even if you are broke, it does not cost you anything to dream of being rich. Many poor people are poor because they have given up on dreaming." —Robert Kiyosaki

- "Ideas are the beginning points of all fortunes." —Napoleon Hill

- "When you are grateful fear disappears and abundance appears." —Anthony Robbins

"Everything in the universe has a purpose. Indeed, the invisible intelligence that flows through everything in a purposeful fashion is also flowing through you." —Dr. Wayne Dyer

- "Gratitude is an attitude that hooks us up to our source of supply. And the more grateful you are, the closer you become to your maker, to the architect of the universe, to the spiritual core of your being. It's a phenomenal lesson." —Bob Proctor

- "Living in Abundance and Success is a Reasonable Option" —Magus Incognito

- "You have a divine right to abundance, and if you are anything less than a millionaire, you haven't had your fair share." —Stuart Wilde

- "Prosperity is not just having things. It is the consciousness that attracts the things. Prosperity is a way of living and thinking, and not just having money or things. Poverty is a way of living and thinking, and not just a lack of money or things." —Eric Butterworth

- "Most folks are about as happy as they make up their minds to be." —Abraham Lincoln

- "And he shall be like a tree planted by the rivers of water, that bringeth forth his fruit in his season; his leaf also shall not wither; and whatsoever he doeth shall prosper." —Psalm 1:3

- "The Constitution only gives people the right to pursue happiness. You have to catch it yourself." —Benjamin Franklin

- "Not what we have But what we enjoy, constitutes our abundance." — Epicurus

- "Gratitude is the vital ingredient in the recipe for Faith" —Magus Incognito

- "We may divide thinkers into those who think for themselves and those who think through others. The latter are the rule and the former the exception. The first are original thinkers in a double sense, and egotists in the noblest meaning of the word." —Arthur Schopenhauer

- "The key to every man is his thought. Sturdy and defiant though he look he has a helm which he obeys, which is the idea after which all his facts are classified. He can only be reformed by showing him a new idea which commands his own." —Ralph Waldo Emerson

- "All truly wise thoughts have been thought already thousands of times; but to make them really ours we must think them over again honestly till they take root in our personal expression." — Johann Wolfgang von Goethe.

- "Great men are they who see that spirituality is stronger than any material force; that thoughts rule the world." —Ralph Waldo Emerson.

- "All that we are is a result of what we have thought." —Buddha

- "Wealth is the slave of a wise man. The master of a fool." —Seneca

- "Happiness is not in the mere possession of money; it lies in the joy of achievement, in the thrill of creative effort." —Franklin D Roosevelt

- "Money is like manure. You have to spread it around or it smells." — J. Paul Getty

- "Liberty is not a means to a higher political end. It is the highest political end." — Lord John Dalberg-Acton

- "We are what we repeatedly do. Excellence, then, is not an act but a habit." — Aristotle

- "Money is like love; it kills slowly and painfully the one who withholds it, and enlivens the other who turns it on his fellow man." — Kahlil Gibran

- "Empty pockets never held anyone back. Only empty heads and empty hearts can do that." —Norman Vincent Peale

- "The thief cometh not, but for to steal, and to kill, and to destroy: I am come that they might have life, and that they might have it more abundantly." —John 10:10, KJV

- "Prosperity is not without many fears and distastes, and adversity is not without comforts and hopes." —Francis Bacon

- "It is health that is real wealth and not pieces of gold and silver." — Mahatma Gandhi

- "Desire is the starting point of all achievement, not a hope, not a wish, but a keen pulsating desire, which transcends everything. When your desires are

strong enough you will appear to possess superhuman powers to achieve."—
Napoleon Hill

- "Move out of your comfort zone. You can only grow if you are willing to feel awkward and uncomfortable when you try something new." — Brian Tracy

- "You can open your mind to prosperity when you realize the true definition of the word: You are prosperous to the degree you are experiencing peace, health and plenty in your world." —Catherine Ponder, *Open Your Mind to Prosperity*

- "There is a science of getting rich and it is an exact science, like algebra or arithmetic. There are certain laws which govern the process of acquiring riches and once these laws are learned and obeyed by anyone, that person will get rich with mathematical certainty." —Wallace D. Wattles

- "Within you right now is the power to do things you never dreamed possible. This power becomes available to you just as soon as you can change your beliefs." —Dr. Maxwell Maltz

Other Readings:

Allen, J. *As You Think.* Novato, CA: New World Library, 1988.
Aurelius, M. *Meditations*, trans. M. Staniforth, London: Penguin, 1964.
The Bhagavad-Gita trans. J. Mascaró, London: Penguin World's Classics, 1973.
Behrend, G. *Your Invisible Power.* Montana: Kessinger Publishing, 1927.

Carnegie, D. *How to Win Friends and Influence People*. New York: Pocket Books, 1994.

Carlson, R. *Don't Sweat the Small Stuff About Money*. New York: Hyperion, 2001.

Chopra, D. *The Seven Spiritual Laws of Success*. London: Bantam Press, 1996.

Collier, R. *Be Rich*. Oak Harbor, Washington: Robert Collier Publishing, 1970.

Coelho, P. *The Alchemist*, trans. Alan R Clarke, London: HarperCollins, 1999.

Covey, S. R. *The 7 Habits of Highly Effective People*. London: Simon & Schuster, 1989.

Dyer, W. *Real Magic: Creating Miracles in Everyday Life*. New York: HarperCollins, 1993.

Eker, T. H. *Secrets of the Millionaire Mind: Mastering the Inner Game of Wealth*. New York: HarperCollins Publishers, 2005.

Emerson, R.W. *Self-Reliance*, New York: Dover Publications, 1993.

Gawain, Shakti. *Creative Visualization*. Novato, CA: New World Library, 1979.

Bishop Bernard Jordan. *The Laws of Thinking: 20 Secrets to Using the Divine Power of Your Mind to Manifest Prosperity."* USA: Hay House and Bishop E. Bernard Jordan, 2007.

Hill, N. *Think and Grow Rich*. New York: Fawcett Crest, 1960.

His Holiness the Dalai Lama, with H. C. Cutler. *The Art of Happiness: A Handbook for Living*. London: Hodder & Stroughton, 1999.

James, W. *The Varieties of Religious Experience*. London: Longman Publishing, 1902.

Jeffers, S. *Feel the Fear and Do It Anyway*, London: Arrow Books, 1991.

Lao Tzu. *Lao-Tzu's Tao Te Ching* translated by T. Freke, London: Piatkus, 2000.

Maltz, M. *Psycho-Cybernetics*. New York. Pocket Books, 1960.

Marden, O. S. *Pushing to the Front, or Success under Difficulties*, Vols. 1–2. Santa Fe, California: Sun Books, 1997.

Mentz, C. W. H. *Masters of the Secrets: And the Science of Getting Rich and Master Key System Expanded: Bestseller Version*. Bloomington, Indiana: Xlibris, 2007.

Mentz, C. W. H. *How to Master Abundance and Prosperity—The Master Key System Decoded*. Bloomington Indiana: Xlibris, 2006.

Mentz, C. W. H. *The Science of Growing Rich*. Bloomington, Indiana: Xlibris, 2005.

Mentz, George S. - *Other Books by Mentz*. Available at http://www.lulu.com/gmentz.

Mulford, P. *Thoughts Are Things: Essays Selected from the White Cross Library*. London: G. Bell and Sons, Ltd., 1908.

Murphy, J. *The Power of Your Subconscious Mind*. New Jersey: Prentice Hall, 1963.

Peale, N.V. *The Power of Positive Thinking*, New York: Ballantine Books, 1996.

Ponder, C. *The Dynamic Laws of Prosperity*. Camarillo, California: DeVorss & Co., 1962.

Price, J. R. *The Abundance Book*. Carlsbad, California: Hay House, 1987.

Roman, S., Packer, D. R. Creating Money: *Attracting Abundance*. Tiburon, California: H. J. Kramer, Inc., published in a joint venture with New World Library, 2008.

Scovell Shinn, F. *The Game of Life and How to Play It*, Saffron Walden, UK: C.W. Daniel, 1998.

Smiles, S. *Self-Help: With Illustrations of Character, Conduct, and Perseverance*. Oxford: Oxford University Press, 2002.

Thoreau, H.D. *Walden and Civil Disobedience*, New York: Penguin, 1986.

Tracy, B. *Maximum Achievement: Strategies and Skills That Will Unlock Your Hidden Powers to Succeed*. New York: Fireside, 1993.

Troward, T. *The Edinburgh Lectures on Mental Science*. New York: Dodd, Mead & Co., 1904.

Wattles, W. D. *Financial Success through the Power of Thought: The Science of Getting Rich*. Rochester, Vermont: Destiny Books, 1976.

Wilkinson, B. *The Prayer of Jabez.* Colorado Springs, CO: Multnamah Publishers, 2000.